*Welcome to your Walking Stick Press guided
journal. Within these pages you'll find:*

instruction to guide you on your way

writing prompts to lead you to your goal

space to record your responses to the prompts—to
map your insights as you heal, grow, and explore

*Along the way, feel free to jot in the margins,
add your own quotes, and let writing take you down
a trail you didn't expect. Enjoy the journey.*

Exploring Your Sexual Self

a guided journal

Joan Mazza

WALKING STICK PRESS
Cincinnati, Ohio

The author of this book does not offer medical advice nor prescribe any medical treatments without the advice of a physician, either directly or indirectly. The intent of the author is only to offer information as a journaling guide that may also be used in cooperation with your physician. In the event you use any of the information in this book for yourself, you are prescribing for yourself, which is your constitutional right, but the author and publisher assume no responsibility for your actions.

Exploring Your Sexual Self: A Guided Journal. Copyright © 2001 by Joan Mazza. Manufactured in the United States of America. All rights reserved. No part of this book may be reproduced in any form or by any electronic or mechanical means including information storage and retrieval systems without permission in writing from the publisher, except by a reviewer, who may quote brief passages in a review. Published by Walking Stick Press, an imprint of F&W Publications, Inc., 1507 Dana Avenue, Cincinnati, Ohio, 45207. (800) 289-0963. First edition.

Visit our Web site at www.writersdigest.com for information on more resources for writers.

To receive a free weekly E-mail newsletter delivering tips and updates about writing and about Writer's Digest products, send an E-mail with "Subscribe Newsletter" in the body of the message to: newsletter-request@writersdigest.com, or register directly at our Web site at www.writersdigest.com.

05   04   03   02   01   5   4   3   2   1

Library of Congress Cataloging in Publication Data

Mazza, Joan.
    Exploring your sexual self: a guided journal / by Joan Mazza.
       p.   cm.
    ISBN 1-58297-055-6 (alk. paper)
       1. Sex instruction. 2. Sexual fantasies. 3. Masturbation. 4. Communication in sex. I. Title.
    HQ56 .M346 2001
    306.7--dc21
                                                             2001017802
                                                                                    CIP

Edited by Jack Heffron, Michelle Howry and Kim Agricola
Cover design by Matthew S. Gaynor
Cover photography by Mamad Mossadegh/Photonica
Production coordinated by Mark Griffin

FOR HEIDI BOEHRINGER

ACKNOWLEDGMENTS

My thanks to my good friends who generously offered to read the manuscript: Lois Avrick, Norma Berkman, Gloria Fisher, Lana Schulman, Cher Souci, and (always) Joyce Sweeney. Thank you for your interest, humor, caring, and terrific suggestions.

My gratitude also goes to all my teachers of human sexuality: Deborah Taj Anapol, Lonnie Barbach, Linda Chapman, Betty Dodson, John Money, and Shantam Nityama. Thank you all for celebrating sexuality and for teaching us to fully embrace our own bodies and each other.

And my heartfelt appreciation to all my extended family at Twin Oaks Community for creating a place where people can truly be who they are in all their individual lovestyles, personalities, philosophies, and beliefs. Thank you for making me feel so much a part of your community when I visit.

ABOUT THE AUTHOR

Joan Mazza is the author of *Dreaming Your Real Self: A Personal Approach to Dream Interpretation* (Perigee/PenguinPutnam, July 1998), *Who's Crazy, Anyway?* (iUniverse, April 2000), *Dream Back Your Life: Transforming Dream Messages Into Life Action—A Practical Guide to Dreams, Daydreams, and Fantasies* (Perigee, July 2000), *From Dreams to Discovery* (Walking Stick Press/Writer's Digest, Nov. 2000), and *Things That Tick Me Off* (Walking Stick Press/Writer's Digest, Nov. 2000). She is also a columnist for *Personal Journaling* magazine, as well as a psychotherapist and licensed mental health counselor with a master's degree in counseling psychology. She conducts ongoing groups in South Florida as well as national seminars on a variety of topics including:

- Journal Writing and Creativity
- Journal Writing as Self-Therapy
- How to Say No With a Smile: Setting Personal Boundaries
- When Life Gives You Lemons . . .
- Creating Personal Rituals and Ceremonies
- Knowing Your Shadow and Subpersonalities
- Conscious Sexuality
- Motivate Yourself!

As a speaker, Joan Mazza offers seminars to professionals and the public, addressing the concerns and frustrations of people in "midlife" crises regardless of age. With humor and personal anecdotes, she invites people to be themselves, take risks, and dream back their lives.

She is a past-president of The Book Group of South Florida, an organization of authors and book industry professionals. Her short stories, articles, poetry, and essays have appeared in many publications.

For more information about the author, visit her Web site at *www.joanmazza.com*.

CONTENTS

Introduction........1

CHAPTER ONE
Journaling About Sex........2

CHAPTER TWO
Firsts........20

CHAPTER THREE
Lovemaps........36

CHAPTER FOUR
Solitary Sex........54

CHAPTER FIVE
Partner Sex........64

CHAPTER SIX
Fantasies........78

CHAPTER SEVEN
The Forbidden Zone........92

CHAPTER EIGHT
Orientation and Identity........106

CHAPTER NINE
Sexual Problems........118

Conclusion........134

Bibliography........135

Introduction

Admit it. You know you want to. Go ahead. Let yourself go. Give in to temptation.

Love is the answer, but while you're waiting for the answer, sex raises some pretty good questions.
Woody Allen

Haven't you always wished you could talk about sex openly, ask questions, and discover your sexual self? Wouldn't it be liberating to let yourself loose without fear?

Now you can—without being embarrassed, ashamed, or anxious; without condoms, foam, diaphragms, or gloves; without fear of arrest, pregnancy, or the risk of a deadly disease—or a disease that only makes you wish you were dead.

Safe sex is here: between the sheets of your personal journal with your writing instrument poised for the plunge. And it's free.

All those years of being told what kind of sex was OK and wasn't OK. And then all those years when you felt you had to prove you weren't cold or scared, uncertain or confused—until you didn't know what you wanted or liked. Now you can write your way to the discovery of your authentic sexual self.

Exploring Your Sexual Self is a special kind of personal chronicle. Beginning with an exploration of your earliest knowledge and sexual experiences, you will discover your preferences, longings, quirks, and perhaps even their origins. By following the writing prompts, you can safely stretch yourself to new possibilities or define your limits. By writing about your most private thoughts and feelings, *you* set the pace and style; *you* decide what you want to write. You can then choose what you want to *do* with what you've learned about yourself—with greater self-awareness and self-understanding.

Step into yourself and enjoy your discoveries.

Journaling About Sex

> *Yield to temptation. It may never pass your way again.*
> Robert A. Heinlein

Your journal is a doorway to your most secret, private self. By writing about your true thoughts and feelings in the context of your experiences, you discover who you really are—all your facets, contradictions, surprises, and deeper inner selves. People journaling for the first time are often surprised at what shows up on the page in front of them—as if someone else wrote the words. But many people who write a daily journal haven't written about their sexual history, preferences, delights, and struggles. By writing and putting these subjects into words, you will understand your sexual self better and clarify fuzzy ideas and feelings.

Organization of the book

Exploring Your Sexual Self is organized to form a logical progression of concepts and subjects, but the logic and organization are my own. They may be different from yours. To get the most out of this book, start at the beginning and move straight through. If you come up against a subject or writing prompt that stumps you, move on to the next one. You can go back and fill in the gaps whenever it feels right to you. On the other hand, you may have bought this book because one chapter snared your interest. In that case, go for it and start there. Do what works best for you.

Orientation

Throughout this book, I have tried to use language that is gender-neutral and gay-friendly, since most people have similar concerns regardless of their sexual identity and orientation. If you identify yourself as a gay person, the chapter on orientation and identity can be about heterosexuality for you. That is, you can examine sexual clues and desires that are counter to your usual sexual preferences and are outside the norms of your circle.

Labels

If you are not sure whether you are gay, straight, bisexual, transsexual, or something else, the text and writing prompts will offer you an honest encounter with your truest self to help you discover other aspects of who you are. Sexuality is different at different times of life, and we may embrace or reject a categorization at a particular time. Some labels feel insulting or mocking. You may experience any label as confining or narrow, and perhaps you will find that *no label* suits you just fine.

> *I came to live in a country I love; some people label me a defector. I have loved men and women in my life; I've been labeled "the bisexual defector." Want to know another secret? I'm even ambidextrous. I don't like labels. Just call me Martina.*
> — Martina Navratilova

Answering the writing prompts

When writing your answers to the questions, answer as completely as possible. Write with the most detail and emotional honesty that you can. By getting to a deep and emotionally truthful place in this personal journal, you will not

> *From childhood on I have had the dream of life lived as a sacrament . . . The dream implied taking life ritually as something holy.*
> —Bernard Berenson

only arrive at greater clarity about your sexual self, but you will also heal some of your wounds. We are all wounded; it comes with growing up human surrounded by other imperfect humans. Let this journal be part of becoming more whole and complete in spite of your disappointments, hurts, and confusion. Have some fun with answering the questions, but also know when to back off and take care of yourself if you feel too emotionally stirred up. Don't expect to do this whole journal in one sitting or even in a week. Take your time.

In all the chapters, feel free to change or reword the question so that you can answer it in a way that suits your preferences and individual needs.

Use the bibliography to further your knowledge about specific issues you would like to learn more about.

Memory

As you read the text and questions in this journal and ponder your answers, many memories will arise. Some of these will be happy, and some less so. Keep in mind that memory is a constructive process—it is never as accurate as we think it is. In fact, the more sure we are of something, the more likely it is that we've distorted the memory. If we have an investment in remembering the event in a certain way (to prove a point or justify our anger), then we will probably unconsciously embellish or change the content of the memory.

If unpleasant memories surface, relax as you write; let the words flow. You always have the choice to decide what meaning you make of what has happened to you and how you interpret your life experiences. When you judge the motivations of others, be aware that you can tell the story many different ways.

Privacy and your journal

All journals are private, personal documents and should be respected as such. A sex journal is not something you would publish. For you to be totally honest with yourself and put into words your most elusive and secret feelings, you can't be concerned about how you might sound to others, whether they might be appalled, excited, or angry by your words. Therefore, your journal must be kept private and you must feel confident that it will not be read by others. Writing a journal is a lot like having a conversation with yourself in your mind. Worrying about eavesdroppers will keep you from speaking your truth. In some ways, your journal may be *more* private than your thoughts. When thinking, we are frequently distracted, or we may deliberately distract ourselves when the content of our minds makes us uncomfortable. By writing, we can follow a thought and its associated feelings along a path and see where it leads. We can stay on a nearly linear path by writing, instead of tripping on our emotions and the uneven pebbles of fragmented ideas.

Sharing or not sharing your sex journal

For these reasons, I strongly recommend that you plan *not* to share your journals—especially a journal about sex and especially at the beginning of this exploration. You will handicap your process by *spectatoring*. That is, you will be watching yourself in a detached and emotionally removed way—even before you begin. That censorship, whether conscious or not, will inhibit the many benefits you can achieve from keeping a journal.

However, as you read the text and answer the writing prompts, you may want to share your discoveries about your sexual self with your lover, spouse, psychotherapist, or closest confidant. Talking about sex with a partner is part of being sexual. Admitting your most private desires and fears can improve your sense of yourself as a separate, authentic person as well as improve emotional intimacy. By talking about what you learn, your sexual relationship with your partner will improve. But rather than share your writing in its entirety, you may want to talk about what you've discovered and come to understand, keeping this very personal journal *personal*: for your eyes only. Too often, in their eagerness to confess, people open up to others who are less than ready for their revelations and insights. Others may be confused by your disclosure or critical toward you with their reactions. Err on the side of privacy—especially until you have completed the journal. A secret revealed can't be taken back.

Think twice before burdening a friend with a secret.
Marlene Dietrich

Securing your journal from children and other prying eyes

If you are concerned about keeping your journal (or this journal in particular) from the eyes of your children, your unease is perfectly appropriate. Your sexual thoughts, practices, and feelings do not belong in the minds of your children. Some would say that even grown children feel disturbed when a parent shares sexual secrets—as if an invisible boundary has been crossed. "I don't need to know that," a healthy adult child might say to a parent.

But young children are naturally curious, and anything "secret" is more delicious and attractive. They will climb, dig, excavate, and demolish to find forbidden knowledge—especially if they suspect the information is related to them in some way, such as the facts of their conception, birth, or parentage.

Perhaps other people in your household or visitors would be interested in the private content of your journals. This, too, may raise your anxiety about writing candidly about sex. While clear norms about privacy and respect for other people's property should be part of any healthy household, the ideal is often not the reality.

You can secure your journal by the same ingenuity that you keep your valuables out of the hands of thieves and dangerous items out of children's reach. Find a place where your child won't go. Consider a lock on a filing cabinet or closet. Some people keep private items in their cars. Some store journals in a safe deposit box. If privacy is so rare in your home, you may have bigger problems to resolve before you can allow yourself to explore your sexual self in writing.

Consider asking for an agreement from family members and designing consequences for any betrayal of trust. And remember, if you don't want your kids snooping in your room, don't snoop in theirs, either. Respect must be given as well as received.

Sexual secrets and fears

Many people have sexual secrets. Sometimes, keeping a secret requires lying. Historically, people have had to lie about being gay or say they were married when they weren't to protect themselves from harassment or unwanted attention. Sometimes, they have lied to protect themselves from violence or the loss of their jobs. Years ago, and in some places today, women had to lie about the children they had outside of marriage or about being sexually experienced at all. Young people lie and say they aren't sexually active when they are. And when people get older, they may say they're sexually active when they no longer are—unless they believe that "old people" (anyone over fifty!) shouldn't still be doing *that*.

Lying is often about shame. If you lie about sex now or have ever lied about it, what shame were you protecting yourself from experiencing? What consequences did you fear? Perhaps these old concerns, which may no longer be relevant, inhibit your writing about sex now.

Taboos

Every culture has taboos. Every era has behavior that is unspeakable as well as forbidden, and every family has its subjects that are never discussed. Sexual taboos about nudity, pleasure, and certain sexual acts are common in many families. The incest taboo is universal, but it is violated in every culture.

Some families never *ever* talk about sex. Other families may talk about sex only in obscure euphemisms or in negative language—referring to its dangers with whispered warnings and tragic stories.

Passion, though a bad regulator, is a powerful spring.
Ralph Waldo Emerson

In your family, maybe sex was not an occasion for joy and celebration. Perhaps the details of sexual functioning—menstruation, puberty, ejaculation, masturbation, and sexual acts—were *absolutely never* spoken of.

These restrictions may have been so much a part of your upbringing that you can't even imagine doing anything that you might have considered taboo for most of your life. These taboos may also inhibit what you feel free to think about and therefore write about today.

Conscious sexuality

Being a conscious sexual person means more than knowing yourself sexually—that is, knowing your preferences, desires, and how to be sexually satisfied. Conscious sexuality also means that you use your knowledge to make responsible and healthy decisions in your behavior and your choice

> *Sharing food with another human being is an intimate act that should not be indulged in lightly.*
> —M.F.K. Fisher

of partners. It means being aware of the more subtle aspects of your personal psychology of sex, much of which you will explore in this book. It also means weighing the risks of your choices and fully considering the possible consequences. Being responsible especially means using effective birth control and not contributing to the spread of disease—from you to others or from others to you. Because you can't usually know whether your partner is a carrier of a sexually transmitted disease (STD), engaging in sex means being knowledgeable and careful about disease transmission. Some sexual behaviors have higher risk than others, especially where there is an exchange of body fluids. "Safe sex" is only comparatively safer than "unsafe sex." The only sex that is disease-proof and pregnancy-proof is masturbation. Therefore, being responsible and careful means staying aware of the risks of each kind of sexual behavior during the height of passion and desire. Staying sober helps you stay aware and take fewer risks.

Prompts

1. Before you begin this journaling book, write down what prompted you to buy it.

2. What did you hope this book would offer you?

3. What would you like to learn about your sexual self?

4. What part of your sexuality seems the most mysterious to you?

5. When you hesitate to write something, what reminder can you give yourself as you write to be as completely honest as you can, both factually and emotionally?

6. What, if anything, about sex distresses you?

7. What part of your sexuality has distressed others?

8. What change would you like to make in your sexual behavior?

9. What change would you like to make in your sexual attitude or thoughts?

10. What change would you like to make in your sexual emotions or feelings?

11. What memories came to mind from the above questions?

12. What do you like most about your current partner? Least?

13. Make three (or more) sexual wishes. Don't hold back!

Exploring Your Sexual Self

Journaling About Sex

How much has to be explored and discarded before reaching the naked flesh of feeling!
Claude Debussy

Journaling About Sex

> Consciousness
> is much more
> than the thorn;
> it is the dagger
> in the flesh.
> Emile M. Cioran

Journaling About Sex

Firsts

We are created as sexual beings by our genetic makeup, our exposure to hormones and chemicals in our mother's womb, and by our earliest experiences, both sexual and non-sexual. These earliest experiences and the way we understand them seem to have an enormous impact on our adult sexual selves. From the start, our ability to enjoy sex, be comfortable in our own bodies, and interact with others in other-than-sexual encounters, are shaped by our *firsts*.

Learning about your body: first questions and answers

As children, we were curious about everything. Before we learned the taboos, we naturally asked questions about the things that puzzled us. Where did we come from? If the baby is inside Mommy's tummy, how did it get there? Did she swallow it? And how is it going to get out? The answers you received to your first questions had a subtext that was communicated in voice, tone, gesture, and facial expressions. These more subtle messages told you what was acceptable or not acceptable to ask. These responses in words and body language may have shaped your acceptance of sexuality as an adult or contributed to any sexual difficulties you may have today.

> *Before the child ever gets to school it will have received crucial, almost irrevocable sex education and this will have been taught by the parents, who are not aware of what they are doing.*
> — Mary Steichen Calderone

Learning about sex

At some point, each of us learned where babies come from. Some of us learned it at home from parents or older siblings, while others went to the library, as I did, and took out books on the subject. Most children learned about sex from their school peers and playmates.

By the time we took a sex education class in school (if we had one), most of us knew the basics—or at least we thought we did. We also had feelings and reactions to this information, based on how we learned, from whom the information came, and how we interpreted it. The emotional context of this first knowledge may have had an impact on adult sexual functioning and the ability to be sexually open and responsive with a partner.

Some children are taught that the *only* purpose of sex is to make babies and that all sex leads to the pain and responsibility of childbearing. If you received this message, you may have had a hard time letting go of these ancient uncomfortable feelings and beliefs—even when you were old enough to know better. Our feelings and our thinking are sometimes at odds.

Learning about passion and sexual desire

Most people learn about the mechanics of sex quite young, but they may not learn anything about sexual desire, arousal, or passion until they experience it. I knew a lot of the details of the mechanics of sex because I read books and was interested in biology. But none of the books available to me at that time (in the late 1950s) said anything about orgasm, pleasure, or the fun of making love and pleasing a partner *and* oneself. When I became a young adult, my discovery of arousal and passion was a pleasant surprise.

Young people today have more opportunities to learn about sex as well as practice what they learn. But for some, technical knowledge and sexual enthusiasm may be widely separated.

First masturbation and orgasm

Masturbation is a normal part of being human. Babies discover their bodies and play with the parts that feel good. They begin masturbating in utero, as seen on sonograms. If they are not punished, discouraged, or traumatized by caregivers for this behavior, they may continue to know that they can give themselves pleasure throughout their lives. Masturbation—to orgasm or not—can be a way to soothe your mood and relax during times of stress. It can also be a way to alleviate physical and emotional pain.

A child's first experience with masturbation and orgasm may color all later experiences, especially if parents make this a shameful or forbidden practice. Your memory of your first experience of masturbation and orgasm—which may be widely separated in time—and how you felt about these experiences had an impact on your adult assessment of both. (See more on masturbation in chapter four.)

First menstruation/First ejaculation

A woman's first menstruation is an important moment. Historically, this event has been celebrated, ignored, or hidden in secret shame. Some girls, unprepared for their first menstruation, believe they are mortally ill and are traumatized by their first bleeding.

In my family, getting your first period meant you were a "lady," and members of my extended family knew which girls had come of age. It was a positive event, something to be proud of, and I recall being very upset that my cousin who was two years younger got her first period long before I did. She was only nine—what nerve!

For boys, their first ejaculation is equivalent to first menstruation in girls in that it marks the passage from childhood into adulthood. Boys, with their sexual equipment external and visible, have usually been playing with their toys since infancy. Therefore, masturbation and first ejaculation is more often widely separated in time.

Some families acknowledge this event with a man-to-man talk (said in a deep and resonant voice). Such a talk might include helpful information, cautions about causing pregnancy and catching disease, warnings and jokes about the lures of women, or a hearty celebration of all that is traditionally manly. In Western culture, a boy's passage into manhood may be nothing more than his mother's silent observation of stains on his sheets or shorts or when he suddenly wants to do his own laundry.

For young people, these life passages are always significant, whether or not they are celebrated or acknowledged. I regret the lack of rituals surrounding these events. (See the novel *The Red Tent* by Anita Diamant for descriptions of celebrating menstruation.)

First exposure to sexual media

Pictures of naked people, movies with sex scenes, sexually explicit films and videos, and "girlie" magazines and playing cards have been around for a long time. I was in elementary school the first time a boy showed me pictures of naked women. I had trouble figuring out what they were. I couldn't imagine why he wanted these pictures or why he was so agitated when he showed them to me and another girl.

The world of pornography and erotic literature is much more open today than in my long-ago innocence. Depending on your age and the culture where you grew up, you may have had more or fewer opportunities to see sexual materials than others. Those first experiences shaped your beliefs and expectations of what it meant to be a sexual person, including your personal meaning of the word *sexy*. As a young person, nonsexual images might have been a turn-on, too, such as watching a rock star or listening to certain kinds of music.

Dirty words

When we talk about *dirty words*, we usually mean sexual words. A *dirty joke* is a sexual joke. Your earliest memories of sexual knowledge may be tied to the first time you used a word that your parents or teachers told you was *bad*. Depending on your family's standards, any words referring to reproduction, sexual anatomy, or sexual activity might have been considered bad words. Their reaction of surprise, anger, shock, or discomfort might have alerted you to the power of these words.

First experiences with others

Children experiment sexually. They are curious to see and touch the private parts of children of both sexes. It is normal for them to want to experiment and see what kissing and touching feels like. Some sex researchers believe that sexual rehearsal play is necessary for normal adult sexual functioning in primates, so such play must also be necessary for *all* the higher primates, including humans.

> *I used to think that anyone doing anything weird was weird. I suddenly realized that anyone doing anything weird wasn't weird at all and it was the people saying they were weird who were weird.*
> Paul McCartney

Your first experiences of sexual play with others contributed to your sense of yourself as a sexual person today. This is true whether the experiences were positive, negative, or neutral.

Some children caught in sexual play are beaten or humiliated by their parents or other adults. Adults uncomfortable with their children's curiosity convey a message that sex is dirty or weird, even if they never say so explicitly. Having been molested by another child may also contribute to a sense of shame about sex as an adult.

If your experimentation was observed by adults and you were punished, shamed, or praised for your curiosity, this event may have had more significance in your sexual consciousness today than you realized. Remembering these earliest events can contribute to knowing your sexual self.

Prompts

1. What were your first questions about sex and gender? List them. Whom did you ask? What were the answers? Were you satisfied with the answers you got? If not, what did you do about that?

2. Do you have any memory of your own toilet training? Describe.

3. What memory do you have of seeing the toilet training of another child in your family? What is your reaction to that memory today?

4. What were you taught about washing yourself? What were you taught about washing your genitals? What words did your family use for your private parts?

5. Were there any taboos that were clear to you without being explicitly stated?

6. How and where did you first learn about the mechanics of sex? How old were you? What was your first reaction to this information?

7. What negative messages, if any, were attached to the technical details of making babies?

8. What was your first experience of masturbation? First arousal?

9. When did you learn about menstruation? Did you feel this information was complete? Describe.

10. When was your first orgasm/ejaculation? What meaning and feelings did you attach to it?

11. What is your earliest memory of sexual play with another child? Playing doctor?

12. What other early memories do you have of sexual knowledge or experience? Write about as many of them as you can remember.

    - Overall, were these experiences mostly positive or negative? Describe.

    - What impact, if any, do you believe these experiences had on your adult sexual preferences and feelings?

    - What can you do today to better understand these early experiences?

13. What experience did you have with sex experimentation before puberty?

    - If you were caught in the act by an adult, what happened?

    - How do you believe this experience influenced your later sexual attitudes and behavior?

14. When and where did you first learn dirty words?

15. Have some fun with dirty words. In six columns for the words on the next page, list all the words you can think of, including slang in English and other languages.

16. How did you feel while making these lists? If you didn't make the lists, what stopped you?

Exploring Your Sexual Self

DIRTY WORDS

Urination	Defecation	Masturbation	Intercourse	Female genitals	Male genitals

Firsts

29

Firsts

131

Learning and sex until rigor mortis.
Maggie Kuhn

35

Lovemaps

Each of us has a unique lovemap, whether we are aware of it or not. We each know what kind of people we find attractive, how we like to be approached and aroused, and the circumstances we find sexually alluring. Even if we never think about it enough to spell it out, we know what we consider sexy or romantic—and those may be different things altogether. Some people find tender romance too chaste to be sexy, but others need romance and sweet words to be turned on.

You can think of your lovemap as all that you find sexually captivating, exciting, and interesting. It includes what you think about when you anticipate being sexual, what you would like to do alone or with your partner, and where and when you'd like to do it. It also includes what you think about *during* a sexual encounter, which may be the fantasies that turn you on or trigger your orgasm, but you wouldn't want to actually *do*. (See chapter six for more on sexual fantasies.)

> Lovemap: A developmental representation or template in the mind and in the brain depicting the idealized lover, the idealized love affair, and the idealized program of sexuoerotic activity projected in imagery or actually engaged in with that lover.
> John Money

Lovemaps are as different as the people who have them. What is sexually arousing to one person may be like ice cubes thrown into the lap of another. What seems like exciting fun in one situation might be terrifying or disgusting in another.

Your reactions have a lot to do with your first experiences and first knowledge that you explored in chapter two. Like many other animals, humans seem to be "imprinted" with certain behaviors, needs, and beliefs early in life. That is, the earliest exposure to sexually and emotionally charged events color many of our later experiences. But because we have a mind that can reflect on our past and present habits, we have some ability to change our programming with education and a desire to change our beliefs about sex. Still, we cannot ignore the weight of early social conditioning—even when we don't remember it.

In some ways, this entire book provides an opportunity to examine the various aspects of your lovemap, not just the questions at the end of this chapter.

Vandalized lovemaps

When parents or other trusted caretakers sexually abuse or humiliate a child for sexual play, normal sexual development may be destroyed—sometimes permanently. John Money discusses specific instances of these disruptions, which he calls "vandalized lovemaps," in several of his books, listed in the bibliography.

Sexual identity

Most of us grow up with a sense of being a boy or a girl. Early on, we learn what we are. Most of us accept that identity, based on the outward appearance of our genitals at birth and what we are taught about who we are by those who raise us. But we also have an internal sexual identity, based on our feelings about ourselves. Sometimes, this sense of self is in contradiction with the outer self—the boy who knows he really is a girl, or the girl who is sure she is a boy or will turn into one when she finally grows a penis. At its most extreme, these individuals might experience their bodies and genitals as alien. Their beliefs may become so strong that they seek surgery to change their gender in adulthood. Your sense of who you are—male or female—will have an impact on your sexual desires and behavior throughout your life.

Sex roles

The culture we grow up in determines what we consider the "correct" behavior for a man or a woman. In addition to the adults in our immediate surroundings, other role models will be those people we see in the movies and on television, public figures in the news, and teachers and mentors. As times change, what it means to be a "real man" or a "real woman" also changes, but our first identification with significant adults will remain with us unless we make a conscious decision to be different.

Sexual orientation/preference

Sexual orientation refers to our interest in other people as sexual partners, not our sense of ourselves as one gender or another, which is sexual identity. Your attraction and ability to be aroused by another person is how you define your sexual orientation—attraction to the same gender, the other gender, or both. See chapter eight for more about gay and bisexual orientation.

Like the rest of your lovemap, your orientation is multicausal. One single event or experience doesn't make a person gay or straight. Explanations that point to single events are too simplistic for something so complex.

Origins of preferences and quirks

The origins of our sexual preferences or quirky desires also have many causes, some of them beyond the reach of memory or biological understanding. Your preferences are yours, and people who tell you that you are weird or abnormal are being disrespectful. If others don't want to do what you like, you might want to negotiate your behavior together, but your preferences are part of who you are. As long as you do not violate the legal rights of others (such as those who are underage or those who are otherwise unable to give consent), you can allow yourself to have your preferences. As long as you don't impose your will on an unwilling partner, there is no reason for you to feel bad about your preferences or to stifle your inner experience of them.

Changing lovemaps with the life cycle

Our lovemaps change as our lives change—as we age, change direction in our lives, have different interests and

> *The more you love, the more you can love—and the more intensely you love. Nor is there any limit on how many you can love. If a person had time enough, he could love all of that majority who are decent and just.*
> — Robert A. Heinlein

concerns, and as our bodies change. What may have been exciting and part of our regular sexual repertoire at one point in our lives may be absent or unthinkable at another. We can choose some of these changes, such as monogamy in a serious, committed relationship or a particular sexual behavior to please a particular partner. Other changes come with age or health problems, such as a reduction in sexual desire.

Intimacy and your lovemap

Sharing your lovemap with a partner and being fully open about your preferences, fantasies, desires, and what brings you to orgasm can increase intimacy. How can you be truly intimate with your lover if you never say what you're thinking and feeling at this most intimate time?

Prompts

1. Have you ever felt as if you were in the body of the wrong gender? If so, what were the circumstances?

2. As a child, did you ever wish you were the other sex? How did this make you feel?

3. What privileges do you feel the other gender has that you would like to have?

4. Do you have any memories of particular events that might have influenced the formation of your lovemap? Describe as many as you can think of.

5. What were you told overtly about the way to be a boy or a girl?

6. What roles were defined strictly by gender in your home growing up? (Did only one gender cook and clean, fix things, take care of the car, or go to work?)

7. What did you know without anyone telling you what was an acceptable sexual orientation?

8. Were you ever attracted to someone of the same sex? Did you tell anyone? How did you feel about these feelings?

9. Do you have any memory of having your lovemap vandalized?

10. Do you have a memory of an event with sexual content that you believe influences your lovemap today?

11. When did you become aware of your sexual orientation and preferences? Write about your earliest memory of these desires.

12. Do you believe people can change their sexual orientation? Explain.

13. Did you ever want to change your sexual orientation?

14. What sexual behavior or thoughts are *necessary* for you to reach orgasm?

15. In the following lines, write the details of your lovemap.

My ideal lover(s): _____

_____

_____

physical characteristics

gender(s)

personality traits

My preferred sexual activities:

Thoughts that trigger my orgasm . . .

What turns me on . . .

What I like: Lights? Privacy? Clothing?

What I dislike . . .

What I would never do . . .

What I'd like to do if I had the chance . . .

What I wish my partner would do . . .

Do you want to change or expand your lovemap? How?

Sexual scales

Kinsey was one of the first people to approach sexuality as a subject suitable for scientific study. He designed a sexual scale of zero to six, with zero being exclusively heterosexual and six being exclusively homosexual. But this one-dimensional rating doesn't differentiate between behavior, appearance, history, and fantasy, nor does it account for changes during the life cycle. Some people have had exclusively homosexual relationships for a time and then exclusively heterosexual ones, or vice versa.

The more we know about sexuality, the more complex we understand it to be. The sexual scales here offer you an opportunity to examine your own sexual style. Keep in mind that this is a snapshot for today. You might respond to the scales differently at another time of your life. None of us are set or permanent—sexually or otherwise. We have a whole range of behavior and feelings.

For the sexual scales on the next page, place an X where you believe you are on the page. If you are uncertain or feel the scale is inadequate to capture your particular preference or feeling, write about this in the blank pages provided in this journal. Also, if responding to these scales has brought up any strong feelings or memories, write about those. This is the time to have your say. The only correct answers are those true for you today. On another day, you might respond differently.

Sexuality scales: 0-6

Place an X where you think you are on the scale. (Only you can say.)

My body is:

| Male | 0 | 1 | 2 | 3 | 4 | 5 | 6 | Female |

My sexual identity (I think of myself as):

| Male | 0 | 1 | 2 | 3 | 4 | 5 | 6 | Female |

My behavior is:

| Heterosexual | 0 | 1 | 2 | 3 | 4 | 5 | 6 | Homosexual |

I like my appearance to be:

| Masculine | 0 | 1 | 2 | 3 | 4 | 5 | 6 | Feminine |

My fantasy life is:

| Heterosexual | 0 | 1 | 2 | 3 | 4 | 5 | 6 | Homosexual |

My relationships are:

| Monogamous | 0 | 1 | 2 | 3 | 4 | 5 | 6 | Polyamorous |

My sexual focus during sex is in my head or in my body:

| In my head | 0 | 1 | 2 | 3 | 4 | 5 | 6 | In my body |

My usual preference is to be:

| Submissive | 0 | 1 | 2 | 3 | 4 | 5 | 6 | Dominant |

I want to masturbate alone:

| Rarely | 0 | 1 | 2 | 3 | 4 | 5 | 6 | Often |

I want sex with a partner:

| Rarely | 0 | 1 | 2 | 3 | 4 | 5 | 6 | Often |

47

Sexual ecstasy is incompatible with hiding your feelings because concealment creates a split in you— preventing you from wholeheartedly participating in lovemaking.
Margo Anand

Lovemaps

Lovemaps

Solitary Sex

Cultural norms for masturbation

Every culture and era has its beliefs and standards about masturbation. At various times, masturbation was considered evil, dangerous, evidence of degeneracy, and was believed to undermine all hope for a healthy future. Children were severely punished for masturbating, and adults were guilt-ridden and tormented by this practice. In some places and cultures today, these beliefs continue.

> *Masturbation: the primary sexual activity of mankind. In the nineteenth century, it was a disease; in the twentieth, it's a cure.*
> — Thomas Szasz

In today's Western society, many of us have been exposed to the knowledge that masturbation is normal, healthy, and may even be a necessary prerequisite for a satisfying sexual relationship with a partner. Some authors go so far as to say that how you feel about masturbation reveals how you really feel about sex in general. Furthermore, they say that placing a taboo on this private activity may be a way to keep people from feeling their own power and being able to control their own lives. Ignorance of our sexual selves keeps us feeling as if we need others to tell us who we are or what we should be.

Celibacy with satisfaction

There are times in our lives when celibacy might seem to be the best choice. Perhaps we don't have a suitable partner, or we need solitude for a while after the loss of a partner. Perhaps our personal circumstances require celibacy for other reasons. These times do not have to be devoid of sexual satisfaction. We can have orgasms alone—without fear of disease, unplanned pregnancy, or having to deal with the desires and feelings of others. Masturbation provides a safe and pleasurable release without negative consequences.

> Don't knock masturbation. At least I'm having sex with somebody I love.
> Woody Allen

Prompts

1. Write down your first three thoughts about masturbation.

2. What were you taught about masturbation as a child? Who was your "teacher"?

3. Was this information communicated to you directly or indirectly? Explain.

4. As a young person, were you ever caught in the act of masturbating? How did you do it?

5. Did your parents or other caretakers forbid you to close or lock your bathroom or bedroom door? What did you think that meant?

6. How do you feel about masturbation as an adult?

7. What guilt or shame, if any, do you harbor about masturbation? What beliefs are behind these feelings? What do you think of those beliefs today?

8. What do you believe about masturbation today?

9. What prompts your desire to masturbate?

10. How and where do you do it?

11. What sexual stimulation do you use? What sounds, smells, textures, and music turn you on?

12. What do you think about while you masturbate?

13. Have you ever shared masturbation with a partner by letting him/her watch you? What was that experience like for you? What was your partner's response?

    - If you have never masturbated with a lover, why not? Would you consider it now?

    - What benefits might there be in allowing a partner to watch you masturbate? What emotional risks?

14. Have you ever discussed masturbation with a lover? Describe.

15. Have you ever discussed masturbation with a friend? Describe.

16. Have you ever discussed masturbation with a family member? Describe.

17. Do you believe you can have celibacy with satisfaction? What personal circumstances in your life might make celibacy attractive?

18. When you are in a satisfying sexual relationship, do you still masturbate? When?

*The truly
sensuous takes
time and a
feeling for the
deliberate,
undulating
rhythms of the
body and
of nature.*
George Leonard

Partner Sex 5

Sexual partnerships are as varied as the people in them. In one partnership, you might be the sexual initiator, the seducer, the kinky one. In another, you might find yourself more shy, reluctant, or cautious while letting the other person take the lead. The kind of partnership you establish with another person will depend on many of the other aspects of your life, including your age, confidence, comfort with your body and sexual desires, and the context in which you live. Like you, your partner brings to the encounter his or her history, experience, beliefs, ignorance, and fears. Each of us contains multitudes, and we may only get to see these other selves with certain people.

Choosing a partner

Your choice of a partner, like your choice of certain sexual behaviors, also depends on who you are at the time of choosing. What choices do you have? What do you want—a lifemate and soulmate or a playmate for a couple of hours? Your criteria for what makes a suitable partner will be influenced by other commitments in your life, your health and level of desire, and your most prominent values at the time of choosing.

If you look back over your sexual experiences, including your earliest memories of sexual partners and playmates, you may see the wide variety of people you are attracted to. Our lovemaps show us that we have specific preferences, but circumstances sway our willingness to depart from our first choice.

Long-term partnerships

Your long-term partnerships can tell you a lot about who you are sexually. Looking at the people with whom you have been with for the longest periods, whether in marriage or other long-term commitments, you can see what draws and holds you. You can examine whether, in your judgment, these partnerships have been good for you and have nurtured your growth, or whether you have stayed out of fear. If you have settled for sexual experiences that have been less than satisfying, what made you do that?

Intimate relationships cannot substitute for a life plan. But to have any meaning or viability at all, a life plan must include intimate relationships.
Harriet Lerner

Jealousy and envy

Most of us have experienced jealousy. Some say it comes from a fear of losing what we have. Similarly, envy is wanting what someone else has. But whether we fear losing what we have or not getting what we want, the feeling isn't pleasant. For some people, jealousy and envy are intertwined and may lead to demands, restrictions, or fights with our partners.

Evolutionary psychologists view jealousy as an expression of our "selfish genes." We want to hold on to our partners to insure their continued commitment in our chil-

> A competent and self-confident person is incapable of jealousy in anything. Jealousy is invariably a symptom of neurotic insecurity.
> Robert A. Heinlein

dren, and we want to be sure that we aren't deceived into raising children that aren't ours. So keeping our partners as if we own them has a biological basis. Others argue that jealousy and its expression is a learned behavior, a product of a culture that treats people like property and equates commitment with ownership. Both of these points of view have their well-articulated arguments. But whether you think jealousy is in the genes or in the culture won't help much when you're feeling it and wondering how to handle it. Answering the writing prompts might help clarify your own jealousy.

Compersion

Compersion is said to be the opposite of jealousy. If jealousy is feeling angry, scared, and threatened by seeing your lover with someone else, then compersion is that warm, fuzzy feeling of happiness when you know your lover is happy and satisfied while having a good time—when he or she is with another lover. Clearly, this is the ideal for nonmonogamous people, but even those who share this view philosophically have a hard time in practice. Compersion is about honoring your lover's right to love others (sexually and nonsexually) without acting as if he or she *belongs* to you.

Polyamory

Some people desire multiple sexual relationships without deceit. Also called *polyamory* or *responsible nonmonogamy*, this love style is *not* about cheating on your partner. Many people who profess to be monogamous have affairs—for an hour or a decade, keeping up the appearance of a faithful relationship while continuing multiple clandestine associations. Polyamory says that partners can agree to have some degree of openness in their primary relationship and can design the rules and limits of other interactions as they see fit. The term *polyamory* encompasses a broad range of relationships, including closed triads (or group marriage) at one extreme, to loving networks of several people, to swinging couples who belong to swing clubs. Each arrangement has its own rules, norms, and styles of decision-making. Polyamorous people may or may not share a household or a continent, income and resources. They might include families with children, gay and straight couples. They may have religious, political, or environmental concerns that their polyamorous relationships support.

Polyamory is only one of many lovestyles and it is not for everyone, just as monogamy doesn't work for everyone. Some people say they have a hard enough time maintaining intimacy in one relationship. Having several sexual relationships may be too complicated, difficult, and time-consuming. You know what is best for you.

Establishing agreements: monogamy or responsible nonmonogamy

Sometimes people make the error of assuming exclusivity in a relationship that has turned sexual, without having discussed this contract. Having been physically intimate, you may expect your partner to be sexually monogamous. Your idea of monogamy might even mean that your partner limits psychological or emotional intimacy with others— telling secrets and sharing confidences with only you.

What is love? What is romance?

These questions have haunted psychologists, philosophers, theologians, and poets for as long as we have had words. Though your idea of what love is and what makes love romantic grows out of your family's teaching, it is also unique to you—as individual as any aspect of your lovemap. Answering these questions for yourself can help you clarify your desire and help you find satisfaction.

Prompts

1. Make a list of your sexual partners and write a few phrases to describe the relationship. What patterns do you see?

2. If you have a sexual partner now, write about this relationship. What works for you in this sexual relationship? What would you like to change?

3. If you are presently in more than one sexual relationship, how do each of your partners satisfy different aspects of your sexual self?

4. Describe what your ideal sexual relationship would look like today.

5. If you have been sexually dissatisfied, what has kept you in the relationship?

6. Are you able to ask your partner for what you want sexually? How do you do that?

7. If you have difficulty asking for what you want, what are you telling yourself that makes asking difficult?

8. What are your sexual limits with your partner?

9. What sexual behavior would or wouldn't you do under certain conditions? Write about those to clarify your boundaries.

10. In what way might your relationship with your partner improve by talking more openly about sex?

11. Recall a time when you felt jealous. Describe the events that brought on your jealousy. What thoughts or feelings *fueled* that jealousy? What was the outcome?

12. When did your behavior spark someone else's jealousy? What happened?

13. What is your understanding of jealousy? How would you like to handle your own jealousy? How do you distinguish between jealousy and envy?

14. Have you ever cheated on a partner with whom you had agreed to be exclusive? How did you feel?

15. What is love? How do you know when you are *in love*? What is romance? What is romantic to *you*? Do you have to have romance in a loving relationship?

*Ideally, couples
need three lives:
one for him,
one for her,
and one for
them together.*
Jacqueline Bisset

Partner Sex 73

*A passionate partnership not only
needs the nourishment sexual
energy provides, it also needs maintenance. Conscious maintenance.*
Charles and Caroline Muir

Partner Sex

75

Partner Sex

77

Fantasies

Sexual fantasies can be a source of pleasure and sexual excitement, or they can cause distress and worry. Your sexual fantasies, whatever their content, have a function in your psychological health, or you wouldn't have them. Whether you want them to come true or wish they would stop because they're troubling, your fantasies are yours, and you might as well make friends with them. Understanding them is a way to understand yourself.

Fantasies as spice

One way to look at sexual fantasies is to see them as *spice*. Knowing what fantasies arouse you and intensify your sexual pleasure, you can call them up at will, enjoying the thoughts and feelings for what they are—only fantasies.

> *I like nonsense—it wakes up the brain cells. Fantasy is a necessary ingredient in living. It's a way of looking at life through the wrong end of a telescope . . . . and that enables you to laugh at all of life's realities.*
> Dr. Seuss

Many people say they have sexual fantasies and a few say they don't. Whatever your pattern, it's normal for you.

However, if you do fantasize, you can use this material to improve your sexual pleasure by focusing on particular fantasies that help you reach orgasm or that increase your interest in the sexual pleasure of you *and* your partner. Fantasizing with your partner about what you would like to do with him or her can be one form of foreplay—first in imagination, then in words. Whether you actually *do* what you've fantasized is separate from the fantasy.

You will likely find you will have favorite fantasies—those that get you very excited and those that reliably trigger orgasm. You might think of these as your personal library of sexual fantasies, available whenever you want them.

No one can give you sexual ecstasy; it comes from within.
Margo Anand

Becoming more sexually experimental (in your mind)

Another benefit of sexual fantasies is permission—they allow you to be sexually experimental within the safety of your own mind. You can "try on" sexual behaviors in your imagination and decide if you want to do them. Maybe the thought of *doing* them is scary, and you'd rather keep them as fantasies. In the fantasy, you have total control over all the variables—what happens, where, who does what, and even the emotional reactions of others. In life, other people have their own agendas. They aren't likely to play out your fantasy according to your mental script—especially if you didn't give them a copy of it. You may also be fantasizing about someone other than your partner, which may be difficult for your partner to appreciate.

Fantasy as a prelude to behavior (mental practice)

Of course, your mental experiments with new sexual behavior can be a kind of mental practice for the actual behavior in waking life. The choice is always yours. Don't assume that your fantasy (or anyone else's) *really* means you want to do it. You may or may not want to take the fantasy into action. Some fantasies—maybe most—are better in imagination than they are in real life, where reality has a tendency to intrude. But if you want to do something you have never done before—sexual or otherwise—mental practice in your imagination can be helpful. If you are considering taking the fantasy into reality, you would do well to include in your fantasy the possible consequences.

Of course, some fantasies can only be in your head, such as imagining you are the opposite gender. Some fantasies may feel "dangerous" because they are in opposition to our belief system, such as a feminist having a fantasy of being tied up during sex.

Sharing fantasies

Your sexual fantasies are very private. Sharing them is your personal choice, based on the person with whom you might share, the nature of your relationship, and the outcome you desire. Some people share sexual fantasies as a regular feature of their lovemaking or as an overture to lovemaking. Others draw a line here and want this aspect of themselves to be theirs alone. Some people are put off by the sexual fantasies of their partners, especially if they contain scenes with other people. "You're in bed with me and you're going to fantasize about someone else? I don't want to hear about that!" Test the waters gently and carefully.

Of course, if sharing fantasy is part of your lovemap and

> *All the works of man have their origin in creative fantasy. What right have we then to depreciate imagination?*
> Carl Gustav Jung

your lover interprets your tales and your desire to tell them as hostile or threatening, then you may have a lover with a lovemap that doesn't match yours. Asking about fantasy and whether your partner wants to share might be one of the topics to discuss *before* you get sexual with someone.

When you find your sexual fantasies troubling

If your sexual fantasies intrude on your thoughts at times when you wish they wouldn't or you find them distressing in any way, you can write them out and try to see them objectively. After all, they are only fantasies. A thought and a deed are not the same. In this era when people talk about the power of our thoughts, remember that this may be only a variation of magical thinking. If we could make things happen by simply thinking them, we would have won the lottery.

However, if your fantasies come unbidden and are consistently troubling and intrusive, or if you fear they are a prelude to inappropriate or illegal behavior, then you can speak with a mental health professional.

Types of fantasies

Sexual fantasies can be divided into five categories:

1. Replaying what you've done and enjoyed (and might do again).

2. Replaying what you've done and enjoyed, but won't do again (because your commitments have changed).

3. Rehearsing what you might like to do in the future (if you have the right opportunity).

4. Running a mental movie of something that excites you but you would never do in reality (because it's dangerous or otherwise unwise).

5. Things you would never do and don't want to even think about.

The first four categories allow you to enjoy the fantasy and separate it from any possibility of taking the fantasy into action. The fifth category includes the troublesome, intrusive fantasies that you haven't given yourself permission to have. Only you know why.

Prompts

1. Can you recall your first discovery of sexual fantasy? What was it about?

2. Write out three of your favorite sexual fantasies. If this is new to you, make one up now.

3. How have you used your sexual fantasies up until now?

4. What began as a fantasy that you later took into action?

5. What sexual fantasies work the best to arouse you?

6. What sexual fantasies bring you to orgasm?

7. Have you shared your sexual fantasies with a friend? What was the reaction?

8. Have you shared your sexual fantasies with a lover? What was the reaction?

9. How important is it for you to share your sexual fantasies? What are your reasons for sharing or not? Does sharing fantasies break their "spell"?

10. What, if anything, do you find distressing about your sexual thoughts or fantasies? Write about that to clarify it for yourself.

11. If someone told you that they find your sexual thoughts or fantasies distressing, what would you say in response to empathize, reassure, or educate?

12. If you could say three things to the world about the nature of your personal sexuality and *really* be heard, understood, and accepted, what would you say?

Fantasies

*Sex is play.
You begin to win
in your sex life
when you come
from this
position.*
Margo Woods

Fantasies

Fantasies

The Forbidden Zone

God forbid that any book should be banned. The practice is as indefensible as infanticide.
Rebecca West

In this chapter, you will explore aspects of sexuality that you might have wondered about, but never experienced. Perhaps you have considered them forbidden or too private to ever acknowledge openly. Perhaps you felt they were off-limits altogether. On the other hand, some of these topics may seem ordinary and not "forbidden" at all. You might even find them ho-hum rather than titillating or thought-provoking. It's your call. Choose what questions you want to explore, knowing this is a private journal and not for public broadcast.

What one person finds exciting, erotic, and deliciously arousing might be offensive or disgusting to someone else. Arguing about whether a book or film is *really* sexually healthy is like trying to tell someone that coffee tastes better with sugar (or not). There is no accounting for taste—in anything—but most of all in matters of sex. After discussing this in various ways with patients, friends, family, and lovers over the years, I'm convinced that our sexual tastes are as individual as our faces, and just as changeable. The pictures and stories that I find very sexy might be exactly what my best friend doesn't want to even hear about, and vice versa. Different strokes for different folks.

Your taste about what is erotic might include certain books and literature. You may prefer explicit descriptions with nothing left to your imagination, or you may like a subtle, romantic, suggestive description of a sexual encounter. What you find exciting is what makes a book erotic to you, not its specific contents.

Some people prefer photos or videos depicting people making love in specific scenes that suit their personal lovemaps. Studies of sexual desire and arousal show that men are more visual than women, with women preferring a story behind the sex scenes. Again, this is highly variable, and even if *most* people like XYZ, it doesn't mean that you should, too. It also doesn't mean there is something wrong with you if you don't like it. Knowing what you like and whether you want to look at pictures or films or read sexy stories—or not—is as much a part of your lovemap as knowing how you want to be touched.

Sexual toys and lubricants add to the variety in a sexual encounter. They can be explored with an experimental attitude, or they can be a part of your regular pattern alone or with a partner. They can introduce a playful mood to a sexual encounter and improve the sexual interest between long-time partners. Some people add sexual spice by wearing costumes (silky robes, uniforms, makeup), play-acting specific roles (playing the take-charge or submissive part), or pretending to be strangers. These variations can be fun as well as safe.

Seeing exotic dancers and strippers can be a turn-on for both men and women. Couples sometimes visit these

> *It's hard for me to get used to these changing times. I can remember when the air was clean and sex was dirty.*
> George Burns

nightspots to liven up their sex lives and increase their desire for one another, returning home with renewed passion.

What you consider "kinky" could be any of the aforementioned behaviors or other behaviors you can think of on your own. These may include specific sexual behaviors—acceptable in your society or not. What is kinky in one time and place may be ho-hum in another. Oral sex, anal sex, bondage, or other activities may be unconventional or ordinary, depending on your ideas and experiences. Usually, what you have *not* done feels kinky.

Other behaviors that may be in the forbidden zone for you might include watching and being watched while being sexual, desiring to cross-dress, being sexual in a public setting, or preferring certain textures, smells, or mental images.

Group sex may be forbidden to you or not forbidden at all, depending on the agreements you have with your partner and your moral values. The very thought may be anathema to you. Or, you may need the thought (or the reality) of group sex to be able to reach orgasm. The same is true for many other sexual practices in the "forbidden zone," including—but not limited to—public nudity, body piercing, tattooing, bondage, spanking, prostitution (as payer or payee), cheating on your agreements (adultery), or going to sex clubs. When you do these behaviors with full consciousness and you share them with your significant other, they are less likely to be a problem than when they are clandestine, secret, and with the risk of unintentional exposure.

Inappropriate partners—by definition—can be a problem, especially when you betray your promises or your loyalty to partners and close friends. Some inappropriate partners, such as those who are underage, can land you behind bars. Exploring your desire doesn't give you license to commit a crime. Sexual fantasy and taking the fantasy into action are very different and have different consequences, as we saw earlier.

Naughty can be nice, safe, and playful. But naughty might also be illegal, dangerous, and coercive. The questions throughout this guided journal offer you an opportunity to be totally honest about your sexual life, beliefs, and feelings in a way that you may have never been before. You may find in it an opportunity to explore the edges of your sexual boundaries.

Let not a man do what his sense of right bids him not to do, nor desire what it forbids him to desire. This is sufficient. The skillful artist will not alter his measures for the sake of a stupid workman.
Mencius, 371BC - 289BC Chinese philosopher

On the other hand, you may be concerned that your desires can lead you to spin out of control. If answering the writing prompts raises very uncomfortable feelings for you, write about those uncomfortable feelings. If you find yourself particularly troubled or anxious, you may feel better discussing some of the issues with a professional. Only you know what's right for you.

Prompts

1. What belongs in the forbidden zone for you?

2. Does visual erotica appeal to you? Explain. What pictures or videos do you like?

3. What erotic books appeal to you?

4. Write your own sexy story for your imaginary video. What are its key erotic components?

5. What do you do that is kinky? What kinky behavior is *too* kinky for you to do?

6. Does the word *kinky* mean the behavior turns you on or off? Does it refer to things you'd like to do or to things that are only acceptable in fantasy? How do you know? What tells you that you can take a desire into action and that another is best left as a fantasy?

7. What sexual behavior would you like to try before you die? How do you think your partner would answer?

8. What sexual activities do you find repulsive or offensive?

9. What is a perversion? Does this word carry a sexual charge for you? How do you decide what is perverted?

10. What's the difference between erotica and pornography?

11. What sexual toys or lubricants would you like to try?

12. Have you ever used spanking or bondage games for sexual arousal? Would you? What was the experience like for you or what do you imagine it to be?

13. How would you like to play-act a different sexual role than your usual one? What costumes might you add to this role-play?

The Forbidden Zone

Forbidden fruit is sweet.
Proverb

Exploring Your Sexual Self

The Forbidden Zone

105

Orientation and Identity

As far as I'm concerned, being any gender is a drag.
Patti Smith

Sexuality varies during our lives. As we grow and become more confident about who we are, we come to know our true thoughts and feelings. We may accept who we are or find it difficult to live openly as we are because of the constraints of our families, social and religious circles, or ethnic group. Gay people often have had a harder time integrating their sexuality than heterosexuals because of discrimination and ignorance. Some people fear their own homosexual feelings because of the interpretation that has been placed on being gay or even having any gay thoughts or feelings at all. Some people fear homosexuality because they have been taught that this is ungodly or a perversion of what is natural. They incorrectly believe that gay people are predatory. Becoming informed about what it means to be gay, knowing gay people, and accepting others as we want to be accepted can help bridge the gaps in this great divide. Understanding comes from knowledge of ourselves and others—without prejudging any single behavior or lifestyle.

Bisexuality

Perhaps even more than gay people, bisexuals have had a harder time gaining acceptance. Heterosexuals may feel uncomfortable around someone who self-identifies as bisexual, assuming bisexuals will jump on anyone. They may be uneasy because they believe bisexuals must be obsessed with sex. Gay people, on the other hand, sometimes discriminate against bisexuals, assuming people who call themselves bi are unwilling to face their gayness. Sexual orientation is on a spectrum. Through growth and development, we move along this spectrum, depending upon our feelings for individual persons and at different times of our lives. No one can tell you what your "real" orientation is; only you know. Any uncertainty or confusion is part of being human. We are not fixed entities in any way—not in our personalities, our desires for company or solitude, our aesthetic tastes, and certainly not as sexual beings.

Transsexuality/transgender

Some people born in the body of one gender feel as if they should have been in the body of the opposite gender. Genetic events before egg and sperm join and during gestation of the developing fetus can contribute to later crises in sexual identity. The fluctuation of hormones for the mother and baby during pregnancy can also create developmental irregularities that result in a child feeling as if he or she got the wrong body. This doesn't mean the person is crazy or unable to "choose" correctly or that they hate the other gender.

> *To me, gender is not physical at all, but is altogether insubstantial. It is soul, perhaps; it is talent, it is environment, it is how one feels, it is light and shade, it is inner music...*
> Jan Morris

Modern medicine has given people the option of changing the gender of their bodies to match the inner sense of gender. People who want to change their gender can undergo psychotherapy to examine the issues involved in making this change. If they want to proceed, they will enter into a course of hormonal treatment and a series of surgeries. Some people choose to live and dress as the gender they feel they are, while choosing not to have a sex change operation.

Most of us have at one time or another felt that we didn't belong or were somehow excluded or improperly matched to our families or communities. Imagine the distress of feeling as if you got the wrong body! Perhaps some version of this is familiar to you. Write about it in the following prompts or add your own prompts to express your feelings or reaction to these ideas.

Prompts

1. What are your feelings about gays and lesbians?

2. What were you taught, if anything, about homosexuals while you were growing up? What do you know now? In your family, what words were used to describe gay people?

3. When were you first aware that some people are attracted to the same sex? Both sexes? What was your first reaction?

4. Do you know gay people? Do you have gay friends? How has this influenced your beliefs and feelings about gay people?

5. Describe in detail your own feelings of attraction to members of your gender. How does it feel to write about this? How do you feel about your feelings?

6. If you identify yourself as gay or bisexual, when did you first arrive at this self-definition?

7. Are you out as gay or bisexual to your family? Friends? Religious group? Employer? Community? If not, what holds you back? When do you feel most accepted being gay or bisexual?

8. If you have not disclosed your sexual orientation, what do you think these people assume about your sexuality? How do you know this?

9. List the names of friends and family members who accept your gay partner(s). If you have children, how well do your family members accept your children?

10. What discrimination have you experienced as a gay or bisexual person?

11. What do people completely misunderstand or what knowledge do they lack about gay or bisexual relationships?

12. In an ideal world, how would gay or bisexual people be able to live?

13. What are your feelings about people who are transgender? How do you relate to their dilemma from your own experience? Have you ever shared their desire or distress?

14. If you could say anything to the world about the nature of your personal sexuality and *really* be heard, understood, and accepted, what would you say? (Note: Does this response differ in any way from your response to the same prompt in chapter six?)

Exploring Your Sexual Self

Orientation and Identity

Exploring Your Sexual Self

*Instead of this
absurd division
into sexes, they
ought to class
people as static
and dynamic.*
Evelyn Waugh

Exploring Your Sexual Self

Orientation and Identity

Exploring Your Sexual Self

Orientation and Identity

Sexual Problems

Anyone who eats three meals a day should understand why cookbooks outsell sex books three to one.
L. M. Boyd

Many things can interfere with sexual pleasure, desire, and satisfaction. These include your emotions at the time of the sexual encounter, past experiences, and the quality of your relationship with your partner. The range of sexual problems and their causes and solutions are beyond the scope of this book, but exploring your problem here will help you better articulate it to a professional if you decide to seek help. Also, clarifying a sexual problem will help you ask for what you want and need with your partner.

How you feel about sex will have an impact on all aspects of the sexual response cycle. Any guilt, anger, fear, or anxiety can interfere with your ability to feel desire, become aroused, reach orgasm, or feel satisfied after an orgasm. If you've just had an argument with your mate and he or she wants to make love, you may not be able to respond the same way you do when you are feeling loving and affectionate. For some, anger heightens arousal and spills over into sexual arousal, but your partner may not feel the same way. Picking a fight so you can kiss and make up is not foreplay for everyone and may be a sign of other problems in the relationship.

Medical conditions such as diabetes and drugs such as blood pressure and psychiatric medications can also interfere with different phases of the sexual response cycle. Alcohol is a drug and may interfere with your ability to stay aroused and reach orgasm. In small quantities, it may reduce your inhibitions, but in larger quantities, it will inhibit your ability to be an active and conscious sex partner. Use of alcohol can also put you at greater risk for contracting an STD, because you are less conscious of the dangers of specific behaviors.

Past experience with a bad lover or a history of rape, incest, or molestation can also be at the root of sexual problems. However, having a sexual problem in adulthood doesn't necessarily mean you have a history of sexual abuse if you don't remember having been abused.

These past experiences can interfere with your ability to relax and let go, which are necessary states to experience orgasm. You may be afraid to trust a partner in a sexual setting. You may feel it takes "too long" to reach an orgasm, or you may feel you come too quickly. You may not be able to reach orgasm with a partner. What's normal?

Discovering what is normal for you is the first step. Masturbation can help you with this, then you and your partner can discuss what you want to change. You or your partner may be feeling unnecessarily inadequate. You might also believe everything is fine while your partner feels there is a sexual problem. Discovering differences in your perception and assessment of your sexual relationship can improve your communication in other areas as well as sex. Nearly all sexual problems can be resolved with education,

Men reach their sexual peak at eighteen. Women reach theirs at forty-five. Do you get the feeling God is playing a practical joke?
Rita Rudner

medication or a change in medication, and a desire to make improvements in your relationship.

When monogamy equals monotony

Having one sexual partner for years often leads to less sex and less novelty. You discover what works for you and you don't do anything new. You may take each other for granted or let other feelings interfere with your sex life. You may be too tired to have sex after your daily routine of work, chores, and bickering.

> *I can't mate in captivity.*
> Gloria Steinem

Monogamy means choosing to have one partner only. That means if you want to keep your sex life exciting, you will have to discover new ways to be exciting to one another. That may be as simple as having sex in a different room of the house or dressing up to stay at home together. Make a date with your partner; hire a baby-sitter so you can be alone with your mate. Your most effective sex organ is between your ears, so just talking about sex and sharing your thoughts can be exciting.

Getting help

Sex therapists are trained in the area of sexual development, sexual behavior, and sexual disorders. They are usually licensed in one of the fields of mental health (counseling, psychology, family therapy, psychiatry, etc.), and they are subject to the ethical principles and standards of the profession. Sex therapists don't watch their clients have sex, and they don't have sex with their clients. If you decide to get help for a sexual problem, be certain the person you see is properly trained and adheres to the laws in your state. You can call your local university or ask your doctor for a referral for professionals in the mental health field. You may need to see a medical doctor first. Your sexual problem may be pain during sexual activity or may be the result of another medical condition such as infection, heart disease, or poor circulation.

Ask questions. Your shyness will keep you from learning what you need to know, and it will keep you from having the sexually satisfying life you deserve.

Books

There are many books available to help you define and resolve your sexual difficulties. Many books can answer your most personal questions about sex. Scan the bibliography at the end of this journal and mark those that interest you.

There are books... which take rank in your life with parents and lovers and passionate experiences, so medicinal, so stringent, so revolutionary, so authoritative.
Ralph Waldo Emerson

Sexual addiction

It has become fashionable for people to call anything they feel passionate about an addiction. However, enjoying sex, wanting to have orgasms, and desiring your partner does not make you a sex addict. Addiction, by definition, means you have a problem with whatever you are doing: Your preoccupation or behavior interferes with your life, you break agreements to get what you want (such as frequently cheating on a mate when you've pledged fidelity), you take unnecessary risks (of pregnancy, disease, or arrest), and you feel ashamed and out of control. Sex addicts usually feel as if they want to stop what they are doing but *can't*.

If you want more sex than your partner does, your partner (or someone else) calling you a sex addict is an unfair characterization. Maybe your level of desire doesn't match your partner's, or you don't have matching lovemaps, so what you want to do seems weird to your partner, or vice versa. Being interested and passionate about sex doesn't make you a sex addict.

If, on the other hand, you feel your sexual behavior is out of control and is dangerous to you or others, if you are engaging in risky behavior that might result in you losing your marriage, your job, the custody of your children, or the respect of your colleagues, then seek professional counsel.

Boundaries, limits, and saying NO

Your body belongs to you. Married people do not own each others' bodies, nor do parents own their children's bodies.

Each of us gets only one body to care for and to decide what we'll do with it. That means we also set our own limits and boundaries about what we are willing or unwilling to do. We don't have to share our bodies or show them in any way that we find unsuitable to our personal sense of what is right for us. We may want to expand our boundaries, but that should always be a personal decision and not coerced by someone else. People who use shame or threats to manipulate us into doing what they want are violating our rights as separate and autonomous human beings.

Sometimes, we feel ambivalent about new sexual behaviors, and we want to be encouraged or seduced by a lover. This ambivalence may result in mixed signals—the classic, "Your mouth says no, but your body says yes." Talking about your ambivalent feelings will help clarify how you and your partner might proceed, taking into account the feelings, desires, and concerns you both have.

You always have the right to say no. Your boundaries are yours to set and should not be directed by someone else—not even someone you love. Those people who can't hear "no" are not respecting you as an individual separate from them. Exploring your boundaries and testing your limits is *your* decision, not one that someone else makes for you.

> *Everyone probably thinks that I'm a raving nymphomaniac, that I have an insatiable sexual appetite, when the truth is I'd rather read a book.*
> Madonna

Prompts

1. What sexual problems have you experienced? Consider each of the different phases of the sexual response cycle when answering this question: desire, arousal, orgasm, and resolution.

    - How might your mate/sexual partner answer this question differently?

2. What historical events such as traumas (rape, incest, molestation) might be interfering with your sexual response today? How have they had an impact? How have you addressed these issues privately? With a professional?

3. How have experiences (or the lack of them) with your previous lovers contributed to a problem in your present relationship?

4. How do you feel *after* being sexual? Explore both your positive and negative feelings and what might be behind them, such as a past experience influencing your present one.

5. What emotions toward your mate might be at the root of your sexual problem(s)?

6. What problems might have a physical basis? Have you sought treatment?

7. What kind of help do you need with a sexual problem (knowledge, permission, clarification, etc.)?

8. If you are in a long-term relationship, what can you do to make your sexual encounters more interesting and exciting?

9. Are you willing to discuss your ideas with your partner? If you hesitate to have this discussion, write about your feelings that make you hesitate and how you might overcome your reluctance.

10. What sexual information do you need? What books in the bibliography might offer such information? Mark them for future investigation or purchase.

11. What do you do sexually that feels dangerous, out of control, or shameful? Is your assessment fair and reasonable?

12. Has anyone ever called you a sex addict? How did you feel? What do you think of that characterization now?

13. Whom can you talk to about your concerns and problems about sex? Whom do you know that is knowledgeable about sex, as well as empathetic and understanding?

14. What is your reaction to getting help from a professional? What are your concerns? Expectations? Fears? Hopes? Wishes?

15. What do you feel was missing in this book for your personal explorations of your sexual self? Write about that now.

16. What is left for you to explore?

Exploring Your Sexual Self

Sexual Problems

I tell you, the great divide is still with us, the awful split: the Us and Them. Like a rubber band tautened to the snapping point, the polarization of the sexes continues, because we lack the courage to face our likenesses and admit to our real need.
Colette Dowling

Sexual Problems

Sexual Problems

Conclusion

> *It is not sex that gives the pleasure, but the lover.*
> Marge Piercy

Sexual sharing allows partners to experience love and intimacy in a physical way that deepens the relationship and the sense of knowing each other. It often provides the connection that helps partners weather the storms of relationship and individual crises. Through knowing yourself sexually and sharing your knowledge with a sensitive and caring partner, you can move toward having the relationship you want—one that will satisfy you and nurture your and your partner's growth to be all you both can be.

Bibliography

Anand, Margo. 1989. *The Art of Sexual Ecstasy: The Path of Sacred Sexuality for Western Lovers*. Tarcher.

Anapol, Deborah. 1992. *Polyamory: The New Love Without Limits*. IntiNet. (www.lovewithoutlimits.com)

Barbach, Lonnie. 1976. *For Yourself: The Fulfillment of Female Sexuality*. Anchor.

———1982. *For Each Other: Sharing Sexual Intimacy*. Anchor.

Blank, Joani, ed. 1996. *First Person Sexual: Women and Men Write About Self-Pleasuring*. Down There Press.

Bornstein, Kate. 1994. *Gender Outlaw: On Men, Women, and the Rest of Us*. Vintage.

Brecher, Ruth, and Edward Brecher. 1966. *An Analysis of Human Sexual Response*. Signet.

Carnes, Patrick. 1992. *Out of the Shadows: Understanding Sexual Addiction*. Hazeldon.

Constantine, Larry, and Joan M. Constantine. 1973. *Group Marriage: Marriages of Three or More People, How and When They Work*. Collier.

DeSalvo, Louise. 1999. *Writing as a Way of Healing: How Telling Our Stories Transforms Our Lives*. Beacon.

Diamond, Jared. 1997. *Why Is Sex Fun? The Evolution of Human Sexuality*. BasicBooks.

Dodson, Betty. 1996. *Sex for One: The Joy of Selfloving*. Crown.

Easton, Dossie, and Catherine Liszt. 1997. *The Ethical Slut: A Guide to Infinite Sexual Possibilities*. Greenery Press.

Friday, Nancy. 1973. *My Secret Garden: Women's Sexual Fantasies*. Pocket.

———1980. *Men in Love: Men's Sexual Fantasies*. Delacorte.

Gottman, John, with Nan Silver.1999. *The Seven Principles for Making Marriage Work*. Crown.

———1994. *Why Marriages Succeed or Fail*. Simon & Schuster.

Hendricks, Gay, and Kathlyn Hendricks. 1990. *Conscious Loving: The Journey to Co-Commitment*. Bantam.

———1997. *The Conscious Heart: Seven Soul-Choices That Create Your Relationship Destiny*. Bantam.

Hendrix, Harville. 1992. *Keeping the Love You Find: A Guide for Singles*. Pocket Books.

———1988. *Getting the Love You Want: A Guide for Couples*. HarperPerennial.

Hutchins, Loraine, and Lani Kaahumanu, eds. 1991. *Bi Any Other Name: Bisexual People Speak Out*. Alyson Books.

Johnson, Robert A. 1991. *Owning Your Own Shadow: Understanding the Dark Side of the Psyche*. HarperSanFrancisco.

Kasl, Charlotte Davis. 1989. *Women, Sex, and Addiction: A Search for Love and Power*. Harper & Row.

Keyes, Ralph. 1995. *The Courage to Write: How Writers Transcend Fear*. Owl/Henry Holt.

Kidder, Rushworth M. 1995. *How Good People Make Tough Choices*. Fireside.

Kurtz, Ernest, and Katherine Ketcham. 1992. *The Spirituality of Imperfection*. Bantam.

Loftus, Elizabeth, and Katherine Ketcham. 1994. *The Myth of Repressed Memory: False Memories and Allegations of Sexual Abuse.* St. Martin's Griffin.

Masters, William, and Virginia Johnson, and Robert Kolodny. 1982. *Human Sexuality.* Little, Brown.

Mazza, Joan. 1998. *Dreaming Your Real Self: A Personal Approach to Dream Interpretation.* Perigee.

—2000. *Who's Crazy, Anyway? (Everything You Always Wanted to Know About the Risks and Benefits of Psychotherapy, but Didn't Want to Have to Pay a Therapist to Find Out).* iUniverse.

—2000. *Dream Back Your Life: Transforming Dream Messages into Life Action—A Practical Guide to Dreams, Daydreams, and Fantasies.* Perigee.

—2000. *From Dreams to Discovery.* Walking Stick Press.

Moir, Anne, and David Jessel. 1991. *Brain Sex: The Real Difference Between Men and Women.* Delta.

Money, John. 1988. *Gay, Straight, and In-Between: The Sexology of Erotic Orientation.* Oxford University Press.

—1999. *The Lovemap Guidebook.* Continuum.

Muir, Charles, and Caroline Muir. 1989. *Tantra: The Art of Conscious Loving.* Mercury House.

Nearing, Ryam. 1992. *Loving More: The Polyfidelity Primer.* PEP Publishing. (www.lovemore.com)

Ofshe, Richard, and Ethan Watters. 1994. *Making Monsters: False Memories, Psychotherapy, and Sexual Hysteria.* Charles Scribner's Sons.

Pennebaker, James. 1997. *Opening Up: The Healing Power of Expressing Emotions.* Guilford.

Qualls-Corbett, Nancy. 1988. *The Sacred Prostitute: Eternal Aspect of the Feminine.* Inner City Books.

Ridley, Matt. 1993. *The Red Queen: Sex and the Evolution of Human Nature.* Penguin.

Sager, Clifford, and Bernice Hunt. 1979. *Intimate Partners: Hidden Patterns in Love Relationships.* McGraw-Hill.

Schimel, Lawrence, and Carol Queen. 1997. *PoMoSexuals: Challenging Assumptions About Gender and Sexuality.* Cleis Press.

Steinberg, David. 1992. *The Erotic Impulse: Honoring the Sensual Self.* Tarcher.

Varrin, Claudia. 1998. *The Art of Sensual Female Dominance: A Guide for Women.* Birch Lane/Carol.

Williams, Donna Marie. 1999. *Sensual Celibacy.* Fireside.

Wright, Robert. 1994. *The Moral Animal: Why We Are the Way We Are: The New Science of Evolutionary Psychology.* Vintage.

Yapko, Michael. 1994. *Suggestions of Abuse: True and False Memories of Childhood Sexual Trauma.* Simon & Schuster.

Zilbergeld, Bernie. 1992. *The New Male Sexuality.* Bantam.

Zweig, Connie, and Jeremiah Abrams, eds. 1991. *Meeting the Shadow: The Hidden Power of the Dark Side of Human Nature.* Tarcher.